READY-TO-GO REPRODUCIBLES
Great Grammar Skill Builders
Grades 2–3

By Linda Ward Beech

SCHOLASTIC
PROFESSIONAL BOOKS

NEW YORK • TORONTO • LONDON • AUCKLAND • SYDNEY
MEXICO CITY • NEW DELHI • HONG KONG

Cover design by Daniel Moreton
Interior design by Solutions by Design, Inc.
Interior illustrations by James Graham Hale

ISBN 0-439-10542-0

CONTENTS

Many children have difficulty with grammar in both oral and written language; but because grammar is a basic tool of communication, it is essential that children master it. The pages in this book offer students practice and reinforcement with key grammar skills and provide opportunities for students to apply grammar concepts in appealing writing assignments. You can use these reproducibles to:

* supplement your language-arts curriculum.

* expand your writing program.

* assign for homework.

* teach or review essential skills.

Using This Book

* Look over the table of contents to determine which pages you wish to use. Choose the ones that meet the needs of your students.

* Read aloud the instructions and answer students' questions.

* If necessary, model how to do the activity. In some cases, you may want to do the first item or two with the class.

Page by Page

Here are suggestions for completing some of the pages.

Page 6   Provide scissors and staplers for students to make these flip books. Have students revisit the books when they are learning about subjects and predicates.

Page 7   Tell students that the words they add are the sentence subjects. Reinforce the concept by having students tell what the subjects do in the sentence.

Page 8   Accept any predicates that make sense. Remind students to end their sentences with a period.

Page 9   Review by having volunteers tell what the subjects and predicates of their sentences are.

Page 10   Encourage students to write a different question for each picture.

Pages 11–12   Review the difference between a statement and a question.

Page 14   Review the words that students color light blue and discuss why they are not nouns.

Page 15   For more practice, have students identify the subject nouns on page 7.

Page 16   Ask students to explain why they didn't add an *-s* to some words.

Page 17   Have students identify the singular form of each word they write.

Page 18 Mention that words such as *and* and *on* are not capitalized. Remind students to add periods after the abbreviations.

Page 20 Have students identify the proper nouns in their stories.

Page 21 Display students' word pictures.

Page 22 Ask students to circle the verbs they use.

Page 24 Ask students to tell what clues they used when they drew their pictures.

Page 25 Supply scissors for this activity. Explain why the tiger uses *am* with the verbs.

Page 26 Have students identify the subjects and predicates in the lines of their poem.

Pages 28–29 Tell students that the best way to learn the forms of irregular verbs is to memorize them.

Pages 30–31 Remind students that they can use two forms for the present tense.

Page 32 Review verb tenses before assigning this page.

Page 34 Students will need crayons for this page. Have students tell which of the underlined words are nouns.

Page 37 Introduce "comparative" and "superlative" adjectives and explain that -er endings are used with comparative adjectives and -est endings with superlative adjectives.

Page 39 Before students begin to write, brainstorm a list of adjectives that they might use.

Page 40 Use the activities to review subjects and predicates.

Page 41 Provide a list of pronouns for students to look for in the story.

Page 43 Point out that the underlined words in the box are prepositions.

Page 46 Have students identify the tense in these sentences.

Page 47 Tell students that the punctuation mark is called an apostrophe.

Name _____ Date _____

Sentence Flip Books

A sentence is a group of words that tells a complete idea.

To make a sentence flip book, cut out the pages below along the dashed lines. Stack the pages and staple them together. Then cut along the dotted line. Match the first part of each sentence to the correct ending.

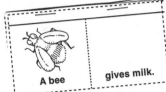

staple here

A bee	gives milk.	**A duck**	oinks.
A horse	lays eggs.	**A cat**	makes honey.
A hen	eats cheese.	**A mouse**	gallops fast.
A pig	quacks.	**A cow**	chases mice.

Name _____ Date _____

Who Does It?

The subject of a sentence tells who or what did something.

Read the sentences below. Look at the picture to find out who or what is doing the action described in the sentence and then write it on the line.

1. A _____ sits in the wagon.

2. A _____ rides in the wagon too.

3. _____ is pulling the wagon.

4. Her _____ wants a ride too.

5. The _____ can carry all the animals.

6. The _____ fly along with them.

Write another sentence about the picture. Underline the subject of the sentence.

_____

Name _____ Date _____

What Happens?

The predicate of a sentence tells what happens.
For each sentence, write an ending that tells what is happening in the picture.

1. The cat _____.

2. A mouse _____.

3. The cat _____.

4. The mouse _____.

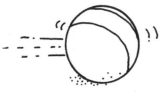

5. The ball _____.

6. The water _____.

Write another sentence about the cat and mouse. Underline the part of the sentence that tells what happens.

_____

READY-TO-GO REPRODUCIBLES

Great Grammar Skill Builders Scholastic Professional Books, 1999

Name _____   Date _____

A Telling Story

A telling sentence begins with a capital letter. It ends with a period.
Read each sentence. Then write another telling sentence about the picture.

Kim plays in the snow.

1. _____ .

Mark helps Kim.

2. _____ .

The snowman is big.

3. _____ .

The birds like the snowman.

4. _____ .

Kim and Mark make a friend for the snowman.

5. _____ .

Check your telling sentences. Did you start each one with a capital letter?
Did you use a period at the end?

Name _____ Date _____

An Asking Story

An asking sentence starts with a capital letter. It ends with a question mark.

Look at each picture. Then write an asking sentence about the picture. We have written one sentence for you.

A Present for Ben

Who put this basket here?

1. _____ .

2. _____ .

3. _____ .

4. _____ .

5. _____ .

Check your asking sentences. Did you start each one with a capital letter? Did you use a question mark at the end?

Great Grammar Skill Builders Scholastic Professional Books, 1999

Name _____ Date _____

Sentence Riddles

You can use telling and asking sentences in riddles. Put a √ next to each telling sentence. Put a O next to the asking sentence. Then answer the riddle and draw a picture of the object.

1. My pages have a lot of numbers.
I help you keep track of days and weeks.
Sometimes I have pictures.
What am I?

_____

2. I am something you wear.
I hide your face.
Sometimes people wear me to a party.
What am I?

_____

3. Now write a riddle of your own. Describe something without naming it.
Use three telling sentences and one asking sentence.

_____

_____

_____

_____

_____

Ask a friend to guess your riddle.

Name _____ Date _____

A Sentence Story

Something has just happened in this picture. What is everyone saying?
Write a telling sentence or an asking sentence for each speech balloon.

1. _____

2. _____

3. _____

4. _____

5. _____

6. _____

Check your sentences. Did you start each one with a capital letter?
Did you use a period or question mark at the end?

 Great Grammar Skill Builders Scholastic Professional Books, 1999

WHAT IS A NOUN?

Name _____ Date _____

A Rebus Story

A noun is a word that names a person, place, or thing.

Read the story. On each blank line, write a noun to name the picture. In the last box, draw your own picture and write its name on the line.

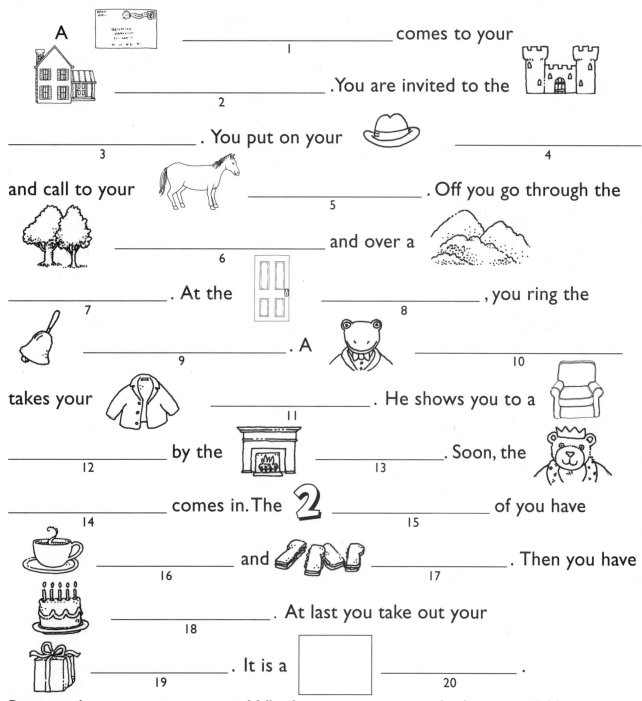

A _____ 1 comes to your _____ 2 . You are invited to the _____ 3 . You put on your _____ 4 and call to your _____ 5 . Off you go through the _____ 6 and over a _____ 7 . At the _____ 8 , you ring the _____ 9 . A _____ 10 takes your _____ 11 . He shows you to a _____ 12 by the _____ 13 . Soon, the _____ 14 comes in. The 2 _____ 15 of you have _____ 16 and _____ 17 . Then you have _____ 18 . At last you take out your _____ 19 . It is a _____ 20 .

Review the nouns you wrote. Which ones name people (or animals)? places? things?

Great Grammar Skill Builders Scholastic Professional Books, 1999

READY-TO-GO REPRODUCIBLES **13**

Name _____ Date _____

A Noun Puzzle

A noun is a word that names a person, place, or thing.

Can you find the hidden picture? Use the color code to color the spaces that have nouns.

Color Code
Nouns that name things = orange
Nouns that name places = green
Nouns that name people or animals = blue
Other words = light blue

Write a sentence using one of the nouns you found.

_____

_____

Great Grammar Skill Builders Scholastic Professional Books, 1999

Name _____ Date _____

Nouns in Sentences

The subject of a sentence is usually a noun.

Choose a word from the tent to use as the subject of each sentence.

shoes   clown

music   car

children   band

1. The _____ sit on the benches in the tent.

2. A small _____ drives into the ring.

3. This funny _____ jumps out.

4. His big _____ flop.

5. The _____ strikes up a tune.

6. Lively _____ fills the tent.

Write a sentence of your own. Use one of the nouns from the tent as the subject.

_____

_____

Name_____ Date_____

More Than One

**A plural noun names more than one person, place, or thing.
To make most nouns plural, add an -s.**

Study the picture. Read the words. Write the plural of the word if there is more than one in the picture.

	One	More than One		One	More than One
1.	girl	_____	**7.**	ball	_____
2.	boy	_____	**8.**	hoop	_____
3.	doll	_____	**9.**	man	_____
4.	lion	_____	**10.**	cap	_____
5.	poster	_____	**11.**	shirt	_____
6.	balloon	_____	**12.**	hand	_____

Write a sentence using one of the plural nouns.

_____

_____

READY-TO-GO REPRODUCIBLES

Great Grammar Skill Builders Scholastic Professional Books, 1999

Name _____ Date _____

Mindy, Mandy, and More Plurals

Add -es to form the plural of nouns that end in -sh, -ch, -x, -s, or -ss.

Mindy and Mandy always try to outdo each other. If Mindy has one peach, Mandy has two. If Mandy buys one shirt, Mindy buys two. Finish this talk between Mindy and Mandy. Write the plural for each word.

1. Mindy: I have a new dress.　　**Mandy:** I have many new _____.

2. Mandy: I will make a sandwich.　　**Mindy:** I will make two _____.

3. Mindy: I saw a red fox.　　**Mandy:** I saw four red _____.

4. Mandy: I bought this dish.　　**Mindy:** I bought these _____.

5. Mindy: I took one bus.　　**Mandy:** I took three _____.

6. Mandy: I will make a guess.　　**Mindy:** I will make a few _____.

7. Mindy: I need one brush.　　**Mandy:** I need several _____.

8. Mandy: I went to the beach.　　**Mindy:** I went to two _____.

9. Mindy: I have a box.　　**Mandy:** I have five _____.

10. Mandy: I planted a bush.　　**Mindy:** I planted two _____.

Write a sentence about Mindy and Mandy using two plurals that end in -es.

_____

_____

_____

Name _____ Date _____

Nouns and Names

Some nouns are proper nouns. They are special names for persons, places, and things. Begin a proper noun with a capital letter.

Study the mailboxes below. Then use the clues to write the correct name for each letter.

1. a letter for a doctor _____

2. a letter for two sisters _____

3. a letter for a beauty shop _____

4. a letter for a husband and wife _____

5. a letter for a pet store _____

6. a letter for a woman _____

Write your own name and address. Use capital letters for the proper nouns.

Great Grammar Skill Builders Scholastic Professional Books, 1999

Name _____ Date _____

Adding Words

A compound noun is made up of two smaller words put together.

cup + cake = cupcake

Can you figure out what these compound nouns are?
Read the clues. Then write the compound noun.

1. A **cloth** that covers a **table** is a _____

2. **Corn** that goes **pop** is _____

3. A **book** for a **cook** is a _____

4. An **apple** made into **sauce** is _____

5. A **cake** with **fruit** in it is a _____

6. **Meat** made into a **ball** is a _____

7. A **melon** with lots of **water** in it is a _____

8. A **berry** that is **blue** is a _____

Write a menu for a meal you would like. Use some compound nouns in your menu.

Name _____   Date _____

A Noun Story

It's fun to hear stories at bedtime. Here's one you can help tell.

Use nouns to finish the first part of the story. Then write your own ending.

_____

Once upon a _____, an old _____ lived in a small

_____. It was near a _____. Every _____,

a strange _____ would come and bring many _____. But, in the

middle of a _____, a large, wrinkled _____ arrived. After that

_____

_____

_____

_____

_____

_____

_____

_____

_____

_____

Write a title for your noun story. Then read the story aloud to a friend. Have
your friend write down all the nouns in your story.

READY·TO·GO REPRODUCIBLES

Great Grammar Skill Builders Scholastic Professional Books, 1999

Name _____ Date _____

Show the Action

A verb is a word that shows what someone or something does. Most verbs show action.

You can have fun by making an action word look like its meaning. Here are word pictures for leap and love. Can you make word pictures of the sentences below? Read each sentence and make a word picture that shows the action of the verb.

L ♡ ve

L e a p

1. The elephants <u>push</u> the logs.

4. They <u>run</u> after the geese.

2. The bunnies <u>hop</u> away.

5. One boy <u>jumps</u> up and down.

3. All the children <u>look</u> at the animals.

6. The tiger <u>sleeps</u> through all the fun.

Show your word pictures to a friend. Have your friend guess and write the verb.

Name_____ Date_____

Things To Do

A verb is a word that tells what someone or something does. Most verbs show action.

Look at these different kinds of lists. Pick one and check it off. Then write 10 things to do for that list. When you are finished, circle the verbs on your list.

Things to do today:
- (Finish) math homework
- (Read) book
- (Practice) piano
- (Play) new computer game!

☐ things to do after supper
☐ things to do with a friend
☐ things to do for a pet
☐ things to do in the snow

☐ things to do during summer
☐ things to do in school
☐ things to do in the park
☐ things to do on a rainy day

1. _____

2. _____

3. _____

4. _____

5. _____

6. _____

7. _____

8. _____

9. _____

10. _____

Choose three of the verbs on your list. Draw a picture to illustrate the action that these verbs describe.

Great Grammar Skill Builders Scholastic Professional Books, 1999

Name _____ Date _____

Verb or Noun?

The meaning of a word often depends on how the word is used. Some words can be used as both verbs and nouns.

Add the word at the left to each sentence pair. Write *verb* or *noun* on the line next to each sentence to show how you used the word.

peel　**1.** The _____ is the cover of an orange. _____

　　　　2. The students _____ their oranges. _____

ride　**3.** Jan's _____ on the camel was bumpy. _____

　　　　4. People _____ on camels in the desert. _____

color　**5.** The twins _____ their pictures. _____

　　　　6. That _____ fades in the sun. _____

smell　**7.** The men _____ smoke. _____

　　　　8. The _____ of flowers fills the air. _____

lock　**9.** The _____ on the box is old. _____

　　　　10. The Turners _____ their door at night. _____

Write sentences using each of the following words as a verb and a noun:
call, ring, turn.

Name _____ Date _____

Draw a Picture

Verbs tell when action takes place. Present-tense verbs tell about action that is happening now. A verb showing the action of one person ends in -s. A verb telling the action of more than one person does not end in -s.

The boy sings.   The boys sing.

In the sentences below, underline each action verb. Then draw a picture that shows the action. Be sure to show if it is one person or animal doing the action or more than one person or animal doing the action.

1. Four birds sit on the fence.	**2.** That dog digs.
3. A man sells hotdogs.	**4.** The girls run.

Choose one of the pictures you drew. Write a short story about it.

Great Grammar Skill Builders Scholastic Professional Books, 1999

Name _____ Date _____

Talking Tiger

Verbs tell when action takes place. Present-tense verbs tell about action that is happening now. Use _am_ or _are_ with present-tense verbs that end in _-ing_.

Help the tiger talk. Cut out the word strip. Cut along the two slits on the tiger's face. Slip the word strip through the slits. Work with a partner. Take turns asking the tiger, "What are you doing?" Move the word strip to make the tiger give different answers. Read the answers aloud.

look
eat
talk
laugh
think
jump
growl
sing
sniff

Write a list of more verbs for your tiger to say.
Make a new strip to use with your tiger.

Name_____ Date_____

A Verb Poem

The poem on this page uses verbs to tell what a basketball player does. Read the poem. Underline the verbs. Then write a verb poem of your own. Your poem can be about a soccer player, a baseball player, a gymnast, or any other type of athlete that you like. Follow the form shown here.

The player runs.
The player dodges.
The player dribbles.
The player shoots.
A score!

_____

_____

_____

_____

_____

_____

_____

_____

Read your poem to a classmate. Can your friend write the verbs?

Great Grammar Skill Builders Scholastic Professional Books, 1999

Name _____ Date _____

A Verb Puzzle

Verbs tell when action takes place. Past-tense verbs tell about action that happened in the past. Most past-tense verbs end in *-ed*.

Write the past tense of each word in the box. Then use the past tense words to complete the puzzle below.

call _____	mix _____	play _____
yell _____	kick_____	help_____
bark _____	climb _____	walk _____

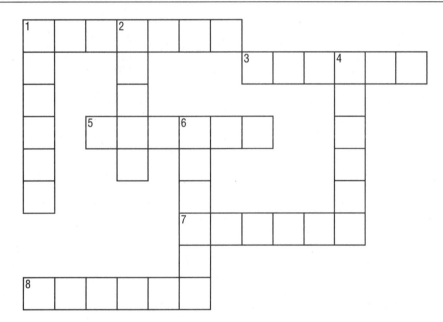

Across

1. Mike _____ over the wall.

3. The dog _____.

5. Our teacher _____ us with the math problems.

7. We _____ at the team to win.

8. The boys _____ home from school.

Down

1. Sam _____ his dad on the phone.

2. Grandma _____ the cake batter.

4. The player _____ the ball.

6. Marie _____ a game with Zack.

Write a sentence using each of the verbs from the puzzle.

Name _____ Date _____

Riddle Fun

**Some verbs are irregular.
Their past tense forms
do not end in -ed. The verbs
in the box are irregular.**

Read each riddle.
Write the answer using one of the
past-tense verbs from the box.
Write a complete sentence.

Present Tense	Past Tense
grow	grew
know	knew
come	came
ride	rode
write	wrote
eat	ate
tell	told
sit	sat
sing	sang

1. I sat on the seat and pushed the pedals with my feet.
I went from my house to the park. What did I do?

I _____ .

2. I was shorter and weighed less last year.
My clothes were smaller too. What did I do?

I _____ .

3. I used my knife and fork.
Soon my plate was empty. What did I do?

I _____ .

4. I got out some paper and a pen.
I thought about what to tell my friend. What did I do?

I _____ .

5. I took a seat and waited.
I stayed in the chair until it was my turn. What did I do?

I _____ .

6. I watched the conductor raise her hands.
I held the music in my hands. What did I do?

I _____ .

Write a riddle using the past tense of an irregular verb.

Great Grammar Skill Builders Scholastic Professional Books, 1999

Name _____ Date _____

Rebus Fun

Some verbs are irregular. Their past-tense forms do not end in -ed.

Write the past tense of a verb for each sentence. The pictures and letters will help you.

1. Wendy ⬚ that race. _____

2. Carl F + L down. _____

3. Shelly ⬚ a good movie. _____

4. We C + ⬚ teams for the game. _____

5. My brother 8 a big lunch. _____

6. We have ⬚ + N here before. _____

Write the present tense of each verb you used in the sentences above.

_____   _____

_____   _____

_____   _____

Name _____   Date _____

Now and Then

Fill in a speech balloon for each pair. Use the past or present tense of the verb.

Past   **Present**

A few years ago, I <u>said</u> "chimley."   Now I <u>say</u> chimney."

1. Last year I <u>learned</u> multiplication.

2. A few years ago, I <u>said</u> "liberry."

3. Last year I <u>read</u> picture books.

4.   Now I <u>jump</u> higher.

5.   This year I <u>am</u> <u>spelling</u> harder words.

6. Last year I <u>wanted</u> a horse.

Check the sentences you wrote. Did you form the past and present of the verbs correctly?

READY-TO-GO REPRODUCIBLES

Name _____ Date _____

Keeping Busy

The tense of a verb tells when the action takes place. Present-tense verbs tell about action that is happening now. Past-tense verbs tell about action that happened in the past. Future-tense verbs tell about action that will happen in the future.

Read the notes on Don's notepad. Then write a sentence to tell about each day. Put the sentences in the correct tense.

YESTERDAY
call Tina
walk the dog

TODAY
buy a hat
walk the dog

TOMORROW
learn 10 spelling words
walk the dog

1. PAST TENSE
Yesterday, Don _____

_____

2. PRESENT TENSE
Today, Don _____

_____

3. FUTURE TENSE
Tomorrow, Don _____

_____

Think of one more thing for Don to do on each day. Then write a sentence using the correct tense for each activity.

Name _____ Date _____

A Verb Story

The verbs in this story make no sense. Circle the verbs. Then rewrite the story with verbs that make sense. You should find 10 verbs.

Alice lost the bread in the kitchen. She boiled the bread. Then she sprinkled jam on it. Alice chewed some juice too.

The schoolbus disappeared at the corner.

"Alice, you will push the bus!"

So Alice quickly dropped her coat. She opened her books into her knapsack and waited out the door.

"Here I reach!"

_____

_____

_____

_____

_____

_____

_____

_____

_____

_____

_____

Make a list of the verbs in your story. Write down the tense for each verb.

Great Grammar Skill Builders Scholastic Professional Books, 1999

Name _____ Date _____

Add an Adjective

An adjective is a word that describes a noun. An adjective often tells what kind or how many.

Look at the noun, *arrow*, at the top of the triangle. Then read each line. The adjectives are underlined. Note how they help to tell more about the arrow.

Complete these triangles. Add adjectives on each line to describe the nouns.

.

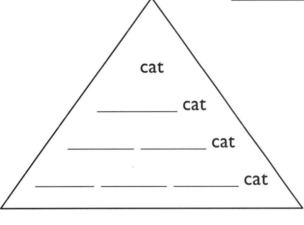

arrow

<u>red</u> arrow

<u>sleek</u> <u>red</u> arrow

<u>straight</u> <u>sleek</u> <u>red</u> arrow

cat

_____ cat

_____ _____ cat

_____ _____ _____ cat

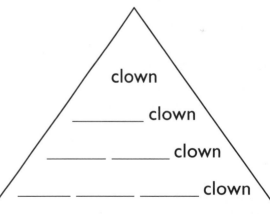

mitten

_____ mitten

_____ _____ mitten

_____ _____ _____ mitten

clown

_____ clown

_____ _____ clown

_____ _____ _____ clown

Write a sentence using the words from one of the triangles on this page.

_____

_____

Great Grammar Skill Builders Scholastic Professional Books, 1999

33

Name_____ Date_____

Adjectives and Nouns

The meaning of a word often depends on how the word is used. Some words can be used as both adjectives and nouns.

What is **orange**?

The fruit is a noun.   The <u>orange</u> is on the table.

The color is an adjective.   The <u>orange</u> cat hissed.

Read each sentence. Decide if the word in the box is a noun or an adjective. If the word is an adjective, color the box with the same color crayon.

1. She wore a | peach | dress to the party.

2. My | gold | ring shines.

3. I got a | tan | at the beach.

4. Her | violet | shirt matched her skirt.

5. I picked a | peach | from the tree.

6. | Silver | is a metal.

7. | Violets | grow in our yard.

8. The miners found | gold. |

9. Molly's | silver | pin broke.

10. A | tan | horse grazed in the field.

For each of these words, write two sentences. Use the word as an adjective in one sentence and a noun in the other.

square

_____

_____

cold

_____

_____

Name _____ Date _____

Describing a Surprise

Use adjectives to describe an object.

Read the words on the box. What do they describe?

_____

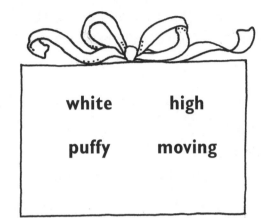

white   high

puffy   moving

Think of a surprise to hide in each box. Then write four adjectives to describe it.

1.

2.

3.

4.

Read your adjectives to a friend. Can your friend guess what the surprise is? If not, can you think of better adjectives?

Name _____ Date _____

Come to Your Senses

Choose one of the types of food listed below. Circle its name on the dish. Then write adjectives to describe how the food smells, tastes, looks, feels, and sounds.

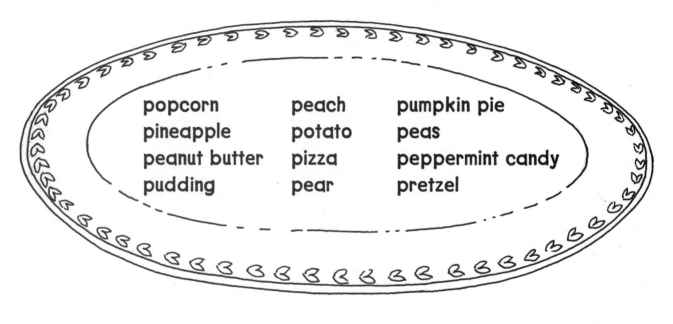

popcorn   peach   pumpkin pie
pineapple   potato   peas
peanut butter pizza   peppermint candy
pudding   pear   pretzel

1. How does the food smell? _____

_____

2. How does it taste? _____

_____

3. How does it look? _____

_____

4. What does it feel like? _____

_____

5. What sound does it make when you cook or eat it? _____

_____

READY-TO-GO REPRODUCIBLES

Great Grammar Skill Builders Scholastic Professional Books, 1999

Name _____ Date _____

Three Nests

You can use adjectives to compare things. To compare two things, add -er to the adjective. To compare three or more things, add -est.

Biddie Bird has a friend named Betty. Betty always wants to outdo Biddie. If Biddie has a *clean* nest, Betty has a *cleaner* nest. Biddie and Betty have another friend named Birdie. She likes to outdo both Biddie and Betty. So she has the *cleanest* nest.

Read the sentences. Then fill in the chart so the correct form of each adjective is under each bird's name.

Biddie	Betty	Birdie
clean	cleaner	cleanest
1. _____	_____	_____
2. _____	_____	_____
3. _____	_____	_____
4. _____	_____	_____
5. _____	_____	_____
6. _____	_____	_____

1. Betty's nest is <u>newer</u> than Biddie's.

2. Biddie has a <u>small</u> nest.

3. Birdie has the <u>warmest</u> nest of all.

4. Biddie's nest is <u>round.</u>

5. Birdie built the <u>neatest</u> nest.

6. Betty has a <u>softer</u> nest than Biddie.

Use the words you wrote on the chart to draw a picture of each bird's nest.

Name_____ Date_____

Adjective Stretch

Some adjectives get used again and again. Good writers try to vary the adjectives they use. Circle the word that describes each animal. Write two other adjectives that might paint a better picture. Then write a sentence about each animal using your adjectives

(nice) dog ___playful___ ___friendly___

1. brown cow _____ _____

_____

2. fat pig _____ _____

_____

3. long snake _____ _____

_____

4. soft kitty _____ _____

_____

5. big elephant _____ _____

_____

6. furry bear _____ _____

_____

7. fast horse _____ _____

_____

8. little mouse _____ _____

_____

38 READY-TO-GO REPRODUCIBLES

Name _____ Date _____

An Adjective Poem

You can use adjectives to write a poem. Follow the form shown here. Choose an object with at least five letters. Write the word vertically on the lines below. Start each line of the poem with one of the letters in the word.

Wonderful timekeeper;
A small reminder.
Terrific and
Cool!
Handy and helpful.

_____

_____

_____

_____

_____

_____

_____

_____

Underline all the adjectives in your poem. Write a title for it.

Name _____ Date _____

Send In the Subs

A pronoun is a word that can take the place of a noun.

The nouns in these sentences need a rest. Pick a pronoun to replace the underlined word(s). Then write the sentence with the pronoun.

Pronoun Subs					
he	you	we	they	it	she

1. <u>Tanya</u> swings the bat.

_____

2. <u>Mr. Bartlet and Mr. Jones</u> blow their whistles.

_____

3. <u>Matt and I</u> warm up.

_____

4. <u>Leo</u> looks for his glove.

_____

5. <u>The ball</u> rolls into the field.

_____

Check your sentences. Did you begin them with a capital letter?

Great Grammar Skill Builders Scholastic Professional Books, 1999

Name_____ Date_____

A Diary

Do you keep a diary? Here's a page from the diary that Goldilocks wrote. Circle all the pronouns she used. Then write your own diary entry. You can write a diary entry from the point of view of one of the Three Bears.

Dear Diary,

Today I went to see the Three Bears. Guess what! They weren't home. I decided to try out their new chairs anyway. Papa Bear's chair was too big. He's a big guy! Mama Bear's chair was too lumpy. She is kind of lumpy too. But Buster Bear's chair was just right. It was really cool. I hope Buster will share it sometimes. After all, we *are* friends. Do you think he will?

Reread your diary page. Circle all the pronouns that you used.

Name _____ Date _____

Where Is It?

A preposition often helps tell where something is.

Study the picture. Find each item in the column on the left. Then draw a line to the words that tell where it is. The prepositions are underlined.

What	**Where**
1. chair	**a.** <u>above</u> the door
2. bear	**b.** <u>on</u> the desk
3. shoe	**c.** <u>under</u> the bed
4. plane	**d.** <u>behind</u> the trash basket
5. cat	**e.** <u>in</u> the bed
6. computer	**f.** <u>at</u> the window
7. dog	**g.** <u>near</u> the desk
8. poster	**h.** <u>over</u> the bed

Pick three objects from the picture and write a complete sentence to tell where each object is.

42 READY-TO-GO REPRODUCIBLES

Name _____ Date _____

Building Better Sentences

You can make sentences grow by adding phrases that tell where or when.

Where		When	
<u>to</u> the store	<u>up</u> the hill	<u>at</u> ten	<u>after</u> the dance
<u>on</u> the top	<u>under</u> the table	<u>for</u> dinner	<u>before</u> bedtime
<u>in</u> the tree	<u>across</u> the field	<u>by</u> the door	<u>from</u> the harbor

The toaster burned the bun.

The toaster burned the bun on the top.

Add phrases from the box to build these sentences.

1. The parade began.

_____

2. The boys pulled the sled.

_____

3. The ocean liner set sail.

_____

4. The taxi stopped quickly.

_____

5. Amanda saw the racoon.

_____

Reread your sentences. Can you add adjectives or other words to make them even better?

Name _____ Date _____

Book Jackets

Use a capital letter for the first, last, and important words in a book title.

What has no arms, but wears a jacket? A book! Choose two titles from the list below. Write them correctly on the blank books. Then add a design to make a good-looking book cover.

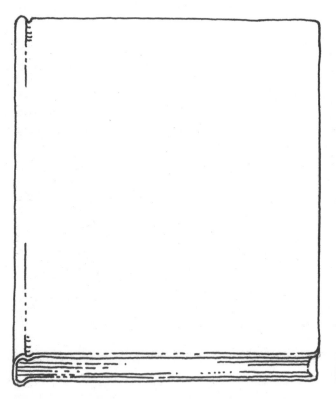

| the spotted cats | greeting card fun | rhino on a roller coaster |
| mystery on seal island | flapdoodle dandy | daisy the wonder dog |

Write a short story to go in your book.

Name _____ Date _____

Title Trouble

Use a capital letter for the first, last, and important words in a book title. Begin a proper name with a capital letter.

Something happened to the books in the library. Can you help fix them?
Write the titles and authors so they are correct.

1. riddles and jokes by ura sillie

_____

2. let's have lunch by ham berger

_____

3. how to catch worms by earl lee bird

_____

4. honey for you by bizz ebee

_____

5. the longest trip by manny daze

_____

6. the big race by hugh wynn

_____

Write a description of what might be in one of these books.

Name_____ Date_____

Who Will Help?

Use quotation marks to show the words that someone says.

Who will help fix this house? Read the speech balloons and write each sentence on the correct line below. Use quotations marks [" "] around the words you write. Then write your own sentence.

1. The painter said, _____

2. The plumber said, _____

3. The gardener said, _____

4. The carpenter said, _____

5. I said, _____

Check your sentences. Did you begin each quote with a capital letter and end it with a period? Did you use quotation marks?

Great Grammar Skill Builders Scholastic Professional Books, 1999

Name_____ Date_____

Whose Is It?

A noun can show who owns something. To do this, add an ['] and -s.

Joe is packing for a trip. He needs to pack everything on the list. Each object belongs to a different family member. Study the picture to learn who owns each thing. Then write it on the suitcase.

skateboard   hat   bone
bowl   sunglasses   teddy bear

1. _____   4. _____

2. _____   5. _____

3. _____   6. _____

Write a story about Joe's family and their trip on the back of this page.

page 6: A bee makes honey. A duck quacks. A horse gallops fast. A cat chases mice. A hen lays eggs. A mouse eats cheese. A pig oinks. A cow gives milk.

page 7: 1. bear 2. panda 3. Jane 4. dog 5. wagon 6. birds

page 8: 1. waits for a mouse. 2. eats cheese. 3. sleeps. 4. has a ball. 5. rolls away. 6. spills.

page 9: Possible: 1. Kim makes a snowman. 2. Mark has sticks and a hat. 3. The snowman has arms. 4. The birds sit on the snowman. 5. It's a snowdog.

page 10: Possible: 1. Why is it here? 2. What does Ben see? 3. What does Ben hear? 4. What is in the basket? 5. Who gave Ben a puppy?

page 11: 1. calendar 2. mask 3. Riddles will vary, but should have three statements and one question.

page 12: Possible: 1. I have the balloon. 2. Why did he take my balloon? 3. I will get you a new one. 4. What are they saying? 5. Do they have nuts? 6. I want one too.

page 13: 1. note or letter 2. house 3. castle 4. hat 5. horse 6. trees or woods 7. mountain 8. door 9. bell 10. waiter or frog 11. coat 12. chair 13. fire 14. prince or bear 15. two 16. tea 17. sandwiches 18. cake 19. gift 20. Answers will vary.

page 14: Nouns that name people or animals—doctor, fish, baby, pig, dog, horse, girl, cat, frog, cow, boy, nurse, teacher; Nouns that name places— city, state, country, town, planet; Nouns that name things—paper, fork, car, desk, bed, dish, book, kite, pen. Picture shows two fish.

page 15: 1. children 2. car 3. clown 4. shoes 5. band 6. music

page 16: Plural nouns—boys, dolls, lions, posters, balloons, balls, caps, shirts, hands

page 17: 1. dresses 2. sandwiches 3. foxes 4. dishes 5. buses 6. guesses 7. brushes 8. beaches 9. boxes 10. bushes

page 18: 1. Dr. Luiz 2. Gail and Bev Lewis 3. Beauty on Broad Street 4. Mr. and Mrs. Green 5. Pet Care 6. Lana Hooper

page 19: 1. tablecloth 2. popcorn 3. cookbook 4. applesauce 5. fruitcake 6. meatball 7. watermelon 8. blueberry

page 20: Stories will vary. Check students' use of nouns.

page 21: Students' word pictures will vary.

page 22: Students' lists will vary. Check their use of verbs.

page 23: 1. noun 2. verb 3. noun 4. verb 5. verb 6. noun 7. verb 8. noun 9. noun 10. verb

page 24: 1. Pictures should show four birds. 2. Pictures should show one dog. 3. Pictures should show one man. 4. Pictures should show more than one girl.

page 26: Students' poems will vary. Check to see that they use four verbs.

page 27: Check to see that students add -ed to each verb in the box. **Across:** 1. climbed 3. barked 5. helped 7. yelled 8. walked; **Down:** 1. called 2. mixed 4. kicked 6. played

page 28: 1. rode 2. grew 3. ate 4. wrote 5. sat 6. sang

page 29: 1. won 2. fell 3. saw 4. chose 5. ate 6. been

page 30: Possible: 1. This year I am learning division. 2. Now I say "library." 3. This year I read chapter books. 4. Last year I jumped pretty high. 5. Last year I spelled hard words. 6. This year I want an elephant.

page 31: 1. Yesterday, Don called Tina and walked the dog. 2. Today, Don is buying (buys) a hat and is walking (walks) the dog. 3. Tomorrow, Don will learn 10 spelling words and will walk the dog.

page 32: Verbs to replace: lost, boiled, sprinkled, chewed, disappeared, will push, dropped, opened, waited, reach

page 33: Students' adjectives will vary.

page 34: 1. peach 2. gold 4. violet 9. silver 10. tan

page 35: cloud. Check to see that students use four adjectives.

page 36: Students' adjectives will vary.

page 37: 1. new, newer, newest 2. small, smaller, smallest 3. warm, warmer, warmest 4. round, rounder, roundest 5. neat, neater, neatest 6. soft, softer, softest

page 38: 1. brown 2. fat 3. long 4. soft 5. big 6. furry 7. fast 8. little 9. nice; Students' adjectives will vary.

page 39: Students' poems will vary. Check their adjectives.

page 40: 1. She 2. They 3. We 4. He 5. It

page 41: Pronouns in diary: I, They, I, He's, She, It, I, it, we, you, he. Students' diary entries will vary. Check their use of pronouns.

page 42: 1. g 2. e 3. d 4. h 5. f 6. b 7. c 8. a

page 43: Possible: 1. The parade began at ten. 2. The boys pulled the sled up the hill. 3. The ocean liner set sail from the harbor. 4. The taxi stopped quickly by the door. 5. Amanda saw the racoon across the field.

page 44: Students' book jackets will vary. Check to see they write the titles correctly: Rhino on a Roller Coaster; The Spotted Cats; Mystery on Seal Island; Greeting Card Fun; Flapdoodle Dandy.

page 45: 1. Riddles and Jokes by Ura Sillie 2. Let's Have Lunch by Ham Berger 3. How to Catch Worms by Earl Lee Bird 4. Honey for You by Bizz Ebee 5. The Longest Trip by Manny Daze 6. The Big Race by Hugh Wynn

page 46: 1. The roofer said, "I will patch the roof." 2. The plumber said, "I will fix the pipes." 3. The gardener said, "I will cut the grass." The carpenter said, "I will fix the door and roof."

page 47: 1. Kevin's skateboard 2. Sam's bowl 3. Dad's sunglasses 4. Mom's hat 5. Fred's bone 6. Emma's teddy bear

READY-TO-GO REPRODUCIBLES

Great Grammar Skill Builders Scholastic Professional Books, 1999